ISBN: 9798376576960
Imprint: Independently published

First Printing: 2023

This coloring book is dedicated to Bethalynne's aunt Norma Jean, the ultimate queen of coloring book kung fu! Many thanks to her for the unwavering support and love—especially in current times when keeping one's spirits up can be an uphill battle. Enjoy auntie!

AtticDryGoods.com

THE RETRO FUTURISTS

Welcome to the third installment of The Attic Shoppe Trading Company's series of coloring books. Last edition we sent you to the bottom of the sea to swim among the creatures living their best watery lives. This time we're traveling with steam powered inventions fast moving towards *The Retro Futurists*.

For us this book means more than just a few pleasant moments of coloring leisure time. All sales for this coloring book go towards shop artist Bethalynne's medical debt as she waits for her turn on the kidney/liver transplant list. As she waits she creates and we are happy to offer those creations to the world as well as being able to take a little of the stress from that medical debt off her shoulders. So thank you! Just deciding to purchase this coloring book has helped with that cause! Now! Please enjoy!

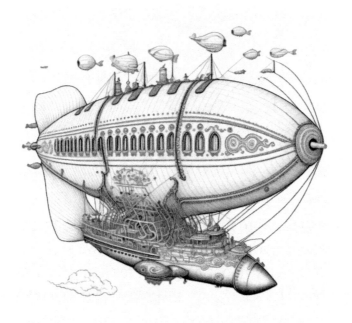

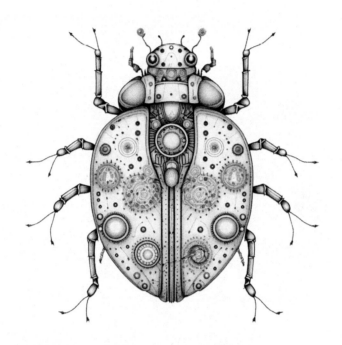

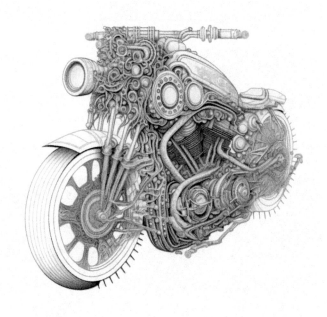

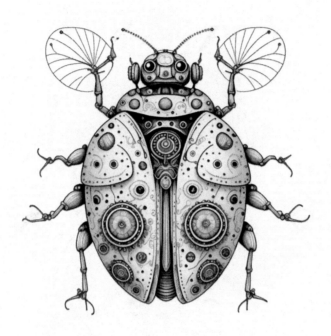

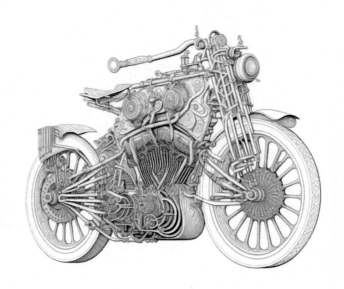

We hoped you enjoyed your trip down the sky roads of tomorrow. Alas we've come to the end of that incredible trip (at least for now – steampunk is always worth a revisit now and then) and all should ready themselves to find their feet squarely back on the ground. Unless, of course, your feet are always not far from floating in the clouds. And if that is where you like to be always remember The Attic Shoppe Trading Co. has a variety of other coloring books and some other neat things you might like. You can stop by www.atticdrygoods.com day or night to see what things we have in our library. Until we meet again thank you again for adopting one of our books and keep on coloring!

COMING SOON: SPRING AND THE FLOWER FAE

Printed in Great Britain
by Amazon